You're Trying Too Hard

The Direct Path to What Already Is

Joey Lott

Copyright © 2016 Joey Lott

All rights reserved.

ISBN: **1517511526**
ISBN-13: **978-1517511524**

CONTENTS

Preface 1

The Direct Path Is Simpler Than You Think 3

Grand Ideas 5

Denying the Existence of Self 7

Agreeing and Disagreeing 9

Manifestation 13

Believing 15

A Deeper Understanding 17

True Lineage 19

Yoga 22

Meditation 24

Entheogens 27

Positive Changes 31

Positive Thinking 35

Being More Present, More Now 38

Being Too in The Mind 41

Needing Time (to Set Aside Time) 43

Shadow 45

Ego 48

Still Feeling Separate/Not Feeling Oneness 50

Choice/Choicelessness 53

Trying to Find "I" or Self 55

Danger Thoughts 57
Stabilization 61
No More Fear 63
"Spiritual" Experience 65
Almost There 68
Living Teacher 70
Diet 72
Intellectual Understanding 74
I Don't Live It Yet 76
Stop Thoughts 78
Being the Observer 80
Have to Get Rid of Illusion 82
Afraid of Disappearing 84
Sadness About No Self 86
Get Another of My Books for Free 88
Please Write a Review of This Book 90

PREFACE

I tried so hard for years and years to attain something that is utterly impossible to attain. And since you're reading this book, I'm guessing that you too have been trying too hard.

There's an amazing thing that happens when you actually remain with what is immediate and direct - what I call direct experience. What happens is that clarity shows itself.

Clarity is always what is. There is only clarity. Yet somehow clarity can seem to be absent. This is only because of a misunderstanding of clarity.

All so-called understanding is actually misunderstanding. That is because clarity is all that is, and all so-called understanding seemingly obscures what is.

So the purpose of this book is simply to examine and dismantle all (mis)understanding. The aim of which is to reveal ever-present clarity.

Clarity is not a state. It is not something other than this.

Clarity is the simplicity of being. Clarity is simply seeing what is as it is.

Clarity is not an attainment. It is merely seeing through what is not true. This is possible in an instant. This is possible right now.

THE DIRECT PATH IS SIMPLER THAN YOU THINK

Just as the title says, you're trying too hard. Any amount of trying is too much. No effort is necessary. In fact, no effort is possible.

If you can truly hear that, then you've already arrived.

If you are still trying, then what follows is an attempt to address some of the major obstacles to recognizing the simplicity of being.

In what follows I address some of the obstacles that I see that keep people stuck in the vicious cycle of identification with a false self. These are drawn from my own experiences with seeking, as well as the questions I receive from others.

I'd also like to offer you this important tip to keep in mind as you read: don't get hung up on the words or trying to understand. If you get hung up on words then you'll just get frustrated. I make no effort to try and present a teaching or use consistent language. That's because in my experience when teachers use language in a consistent way then seekers tend to give meanings to the words.

I know that I used to do that.

And it's not helpful. Because none of this *means* anything. All of it is merely to point to what is unavoidable. All of it is an invitation to remain with direct experience, by which I simply mean non-conceptual sensory perception.

That's all.

GRAND IDEAS

Years ago I used to attend a meditation group led by a self-proclaimed spiritually-enlightened teacher. He claimed to transmit Shaktipat as we sat with our eyes closed in meditation. Afterward there would be a talk and we could ask our questions.

There was a guy named Joe who frequented the meetings. There was something different about Joe. I'm guessing he could get an easy autism diagnosis.

Joe carried a street map that he consulted often. This was an interesting metaphor because Joe seemed to be constantly trying to get everything to fit with his internal map of reality.

The teacher, a guy who called himself Aham Brahmasmi, would speak of Brahman or spiritual enlightenment and Joe would frequently interrupt to ask if Aham was referring to "cosmic consciousness."

Joe had evidently learned about cosmic consciousness at some point. This was his point of reference. He had cosmic consciousness clearly marked on his map.

Joe was a special case. But only in that he was so overt in his attempts to make everything fit his ideas.

I was doing the same. I didn't feel the need to interrupt Aham and clarify terms. But that was only because I was able to translate on my own.

"Brahman" = my idea of what that means.

"Spiritual enlightenment" = my idea of what that means.

See how you do this too.

When you read these words, see how you think you know what they mean. See how you translate them to your own ideas of what things mean.

The only trouble with this is that none of it means anything.

Your ideas are merely that: ideas. They don't mean anything. There is no Brahman. There is no spiritual enlightenment. The ideas of what you think any of this means are not the truth. They are not the reality. They are just ideas.

Ideas will never give you what you want. You want the simplicity of being. The peace that surpasses understanding. The reality of what is.

What you seek is unavoidable. What you seek is what is. Already. This.

DENYING THE EXISTENCE OF SELF

At some point I encountered the idea of the illusion of a separate self. I turned this into a thing to attain. I tried to attain this by denying the existence of a separate self. I tried to be no one.

I see others making this same mistake frequently.

You cannot become no one. Any attempts to become no one will backfire. Because the attempts to become no one presuppose that there is someone in the first place.

There is no separate individual. This is reality. This is what is found in direct experience.

But you cannot do this. You cannot create this. You cannot change your experience to become an experience of no separate self.

The experience of no separate self is not different from this.

This is already it.

Turn to direct experience right now. Can you find a separate self? Look to see where is the one that you call yourself? Where are the boundaries of this that you call yourself?

Can you find it?

This is it. It is not a new idea. It is not a new experience. It is not a new attainment.

It is just this. Simply see this clearly. Cease the delusion.

That is all.

AGREEING AND DISAGREEING

When I was seeking I must have read 50 books on the subject of non-duality. I somehow imagined that what I needed was to acquire more information. My delusion was that by merely reading more books I would encounter the missing pieces of information that would complete my understanding.

This is, of course, rather fundamentally flawed.

There is no understanding possible. Understanding is just the illusion that seems to obscure clear seeing.

When you read a book such as this or when you attend a meeting with a teacher of non-duality, notice how you agree or disagree with what is said.

Can you see how you attempt to fit what you hear into your model of what is?

Models are not the same as what is. And this is the cause of suffering.

What is, *is*. It requires no model. It requires no agreement or disagreement.

In fact, agreement or disagreement is merely what is. Can you see the pointlessness and futility of trying to model reality?

Notice that all agreement and disagreement require comparison. You can only agree or disagree relative to something else. Agreement and disagreement require more than one. Without two or more it is impossible to agree or disagree.

Notice that agreement and disagreement require time. You can only agree or disagree by comparing present thoughts with prior thoughts.

Which is all completely fictional. Because there is only this. There is nothing apart from this.

Right now look only to direct experience. Refuse to accept a thought as an answer. Refuse to compare or try to understand. And instead, simply look to direct experience to see if you can find anything other than this.

What do I mean by "this?" Just this. Whatever this is. Exactly as it is. This right now. Before thought. Before concept. Just this. Whatever is found in direct experience.

In direct experience can you agree or disagree? What would you be agreeing or disagreeing with?

Notice that agreement and disagreement are just thought compared with thought. They have nothing whatsoever to do with direct experience. They have nothing to do with anything. They appear to be about something. Yet actually, they're just thought compared to thought. It's just thought.

It's meaningless.

What you are truly seeking is that which cannot be found. You cannot find this because this is all that is. It isn't hidden. It isn't missing. It is all that is.

Agreeing and disagreeing cannot affect this. Agreeing and disagreeing can only seemingly obscure this.

What you are seeking is so much simpler than agreement or disagreement that the very act of looking to thought to find an answer causes you to overlook what is closer and more immediate.

As you read this, make no attempt to agree or disagree. Or, if you must, then disagree with what you agree with and agree with what you disagree with. At least start to see the meaninglessness of all the effort to understand.

Understanding will not give you what you seek. What you seek is this. You cannot understand this. This is already evident. It is this. Exactly as it is right now.

I am not suggesting that this is a thing. It is not. This is not a thing. That is why you cannot understand it. It is just this.

Stop trying to find it. It is this. Right now. Sounds. Sensations. Thoughts. Feelings. Memories. Doubts. Ideas. Concepts. You. Me. Words. This. The direct experience of this. Before the concepts, yet including the concepts.

You agree or disagree because you want to reinforce your model of reality. Your model of reality is useless. Worse than useless. It is suffering.

What is closer than agreeing or disagreeing? Where do agreement and disagreement come from? Can you find the source of agreement and disagreement?

MANIFESTATION

When I first discovered non-duality, I was immediately attracted to it. But I had a conflict: how to reconcile non-duality with manifestation.

There is, of course, nothing to reconcile. There is only this.

Nonetheless, this seems to be one of the major stumbling blocks that seekers encounter time and time again.

The problem is entirely conceptual. It is because you have an idea of what non-duality means. And you have an idea of what manifestation means. And your ideas appear to be irreconcilable.

Fundamentally, this comes back down to an attempt to understand that which defies understanding. If you can understand it, then it is not "it". That which you can understand is a concept. What you are seeking to understand is not a concept. Therefore, you will always fail to understand.

What I point to when I say things such as non-duality or the simplicity of being is not a thing. It is this. Exactly this. Right now. Nothing other than this. Because this is all that is.

Truly, you cannot understand this. So you must employ a different strategy.

The frustration can arise because you think that understanding is the only way. But you are mistaken.

Direct experience is the way.

Look to direct experience right now. This is absolutely effortless. There is no trying required. Why? Because direct experience is unavoidable. It is what is happening.

The easiest way that I know of to "find" direct experience (which, of course, is unfindable since it is already what is) is to notice what is happening. Notice that this is happening already before any thought or name or label or concept or idea.

Notice that you experience sensation before the label for the sensation arises. Notice that you see color and shape before the name for an object arises. This is already happening. Simply remain with this. Refuse to accept any thought or concept or idea or label as an answer.

Allow thought to happen. Give no special attention to it. Just notice what is already happening.

From direct experience can you find any distinction between form and formlessness? Can you find any distinction between emptiness and fullness? Can you find any boundaries whatsoever?

BELIEVING

Believe it or not, belief is completely meaningless. Belief is merely belief. Nothing more.

Yet we live in a culture that seems to value belief immensely. As such, it is hardly a surprise that so many of us are mesmerized by belief.

There is nothing wrong with belief. It's just that belief has absolutely nothing to do with the simplicity of being. And so seeking for the simplicity of being, which is to say, seeking for freedom by forming and holding to beliefs is a flawed strategy that is doomed to failure.

While there is nothing wrong with belief, the fixation on belief seems to obscure the clarity of the simplicity of being.

Belief is merely a thought or idea that is held to be true. No thought or idea is true. This is the flaw.

In fact, in direct experience, no thought or idea can be found.

I used to puzzle at the (misleading) statements of sages and teachers claiming that upon realizing the simplicity of being their minds became silent.

This is misleading because it is open to misinterpretation - the notion that it is possible to silence or stop thought.

You cannot stop thought.

Yet you can remain with direct experience. You can do this right now. Simply refuse to accept a thought or name or label or concept as an answer. Remain with what is unavoidable. Whatever is happening. Just remain with this exactly as it is. The direct experience.

Here it is impossible to find any thought. Here it is impossible to find any belief. This is before belief. Beyond belief. This is what already is.

Belief cannot give you what already is. Belief can merely obscure that clarity of ever-present reality, which is non-conceptual.

A DEEPER UNDERSTANDING

I remember sitting in meetings with Gangaji and thinking that if I could only hear the deeper meaning of her words then I would finally wake up and be free.

I sat in meetings with Wayne Liquorman and thought that if I could only hear the deeper meaning of his words then I would finally wake up and be free.

I went to more Gangaji meetings than Wayne Liquorman meetings. Largely, I suspect, because Gangaji offered more opportunity for me to believe there was deeper meaning. Wayne offered little to nothing in that regard. He tore down every attempt to find meaning - deeper or otherwise.

The trouble with trying to hear the deeper meaning is that there is none. There is no meaning.

The truest teachings are those that offer no meaning and give you little opportunity to seek for meaning. The truest teachings remove meaning.

In retrospect, the search for a deeper understanding was the only obstacle to awakening to the simplicity of being. Awakening to the simplicity of being is not an understanding - deep, shallow, or otherwise.

Understanding is of absolutely no use to you if what you seek is freedom. Freedom is the freedom of what is exactly as it is - before, during, and after supposed understanding.

Understanding is conceptual. When you understand, you "wrap your head around" something.

You cannot wrap your head around what is. Thoughts are what is. Or, rather, what is includes so-called thoughts. Thoughts cannot capture what is. Hopefully this is obvious now.

Right now, imagine what deeper understanding will give you. What is it that you seek through deeper understanding? Is deeper understanding your end goal? If not, the take the shortcut. Go directly to that which you most deeply long for.

What is it that you most deeply long for? Is it not true freedom? What you most deeply long for is the simplicity of being.

The simplicity of being is so utterly simple that to even move in the direction of understanding is to move away from it. Which is, of course, not strictly, literally true since there is no movement other than seeming movement in and as the simplicity of being.

There is only this. There is nothing other than this. Any attempt to understand merely obscures the simplicity of this.

Give up understanding.

TRUE LINEAGE

I used to play a funny game. It's the lineage game. It's the "is my teacher pure enough" game.

Upon awakening to the simplicity of being it is obvious that the whole lineage game is utter nonsense. It is meaningless.

In case you don't know what I mean by the lineage game, I'll explain.

Wayne Liquorman has credentials. His teacher, Ramesh Balsekar, was reportedly a direct student of Nisargadatta Maharaj. Nisargadatta is generally recognized to have been a fully realized being (whatever that means.)

Can you see how completely ridiculous this is?

Gangaji has credentials. For one thing, her name is Gangaji, which in and of itself suggests authority. Her teacher, H. W. L. Poonja, a.k.a. Papaji, was said to have been a direct disciple of Ramana Maharshi. Ramana Maharshi is generally recognized to have been a fully realized being (whatever that means).

Seriously. Can you see how meaningless this is?

I had doubts, though. I could never be sure. I mean, I was certain (by which I mean I held the unexamined belief) that Nisargadatta and Ramana were the real deal. (There is no "real deal." There is only this.) After all, 50,000 Elvis fans can't be wrong.

But Ramesh is said to have gone a little crazy there toward the end. It's reported that he didn't teach "pure" non-duality in the last few years.

And Papaji wasn't always so clear either. Plus, Papaji sent out dozens of highly-suspect disciples of his own.

So then the search would continue. For the pure teacher of pure lineage.

Yogananda had a pretty impeccable lineage. Except that there's no way to confirm it. And then, Yogananda's teaching was all over the place. At times he sounded like a New Thought minister rather than someone awakened to the simplicity of being.

So then what? Where's the perfect teacher from the perfect lineage?

Lineage is meaningless.

Really.

I promise.

Give it up.

There's no transmission.

There's no magical spiritual energy.

There's only this.

There is nothing else.

And no lineage can offer you this. This is what is. Simply drop your search for something else.

YOGA

I know someone who believed that yoga saved her life.

She had been placed in a psychiatric ward against her will with a diagnosis of a psychotic break. She heard voices. Long-term crack cocaine and heroin use were involved.

She discovered yoga in the hospital.

She sobered up.

Yoga had changed her life.

I got introduced to yoga through Anusara yoga in 2000.

I just learned that last year a scandal blew up around Anusara yoga founder, Jon Friend.

Apparently he smoked marijuana and had sex magick ceremonies with consenting adults.

The problem is that people think that yoga is important.

It's not. It's just yoga.

And yes, I'm talking about all of it. Hatha. Jnana. Bhakti.

Karma. Kriya. Raja.

It's just yoga. It's nothing to do with the simplicity of being. It's not important. It is meaningless.

Do you agree with this? Disagree with this? Can you see how your beliefs and your agreement or disagreement are meaningless and futile?

Yoga is just yoga. Despite what you may believe.

The simplicity of being is what already is. You don't need to do anything to get it. You don't need any special conditions to see it. You don't need to purify yourself. You don't need to do anything. Any doing (seemingly) obscures the clarity of what is as it is.

MEDITATION

Aham Brahmasmi gave me a mantra. I've written about this elsewhere. So you may know about it already.

At first my meditations were awesome. I saw the currents of creation. I touched upon the blue pearl of the ultimate reality. My sense of self expanded and dissolved until I was one with all that is.

And then I hit a plateau. I needed more.

I tried lots of other things. Including buying a lifetime subscription to HoloSync, one of the original binaural beats meditation programs (perhaps second to the Monroe Institute).

HoloSync is set up with 12 levels. You know when you've "graduated" from one level to the next when the meditations at that level no longer have the same effect.

More. More. More.

Nothing wrong with that, of course.

But it has nothing to do with the simplicity of being.

When I got really sick about three years ago, I started smoking a lot of pot.

Cannabis was awesome at first. I was totally blissed out. I was the merging of Shiva and Shakti.

Sort of like meditation.

And then I needed more. And more. And more.

Nothing wrong with that, of course.

But it has nothing to do with the simplicity of being.

Meditation is a state. Just like a marijuana high is a state. Just like sleeping is a state. Just like orgasm is a state. Just like hungry is a state.

States come and go. States happen in the simplicity of being. The simplicity of being is completely unaffected by states.

The simplicity of being is what is regardless of states. It doesn't matter how good or bad the states are. It doesn't matter how advanced or remedial the states are. States are completely irrelevant to the simplicity of being.

It doesn't matter how long you've been meditating. It doesn't matter how advanced your meditation is. It doesn't matter how profound your meditative experiences are. It doesn't matter whether you can cognize consciousness or not. It doesn't matter whether your guru has told you that you are "almost there" or not.

None of it matters. It is completely meaningless.

Meditation is merely meditation. Nothing more. It doesn't mean anything. It doesn't give you anything. And it most certainly cannot give you freedom or the simplicity of being.

Freedom, which is the simplicity of being, is what is regardless of anything else.

Sometimes non-duality teachers will speak of "true" meditation as the simple awareness of what is as it is. Which is fine. And it points to the simplicity of being.

But it is not the simplicity of being. Nor will it give you the simplicity of being.

Because you think it means something. And it doesn't. It's just a pointing from nothingness to nothingness. There is no way to get here. This is already it. You cannot get to what already is.

What is, is unavoidable. Meditation - "true" or otherwise - cannot give you this. "True" meditation is merely pointing to the unavoidability of what is. Simply recognize this. Stop searching for something else. And no meditation is necessary.

ENTHEOGENS

I went through an entheogen kick.

If you're not familiar with the term, it's a fancy term that sounds more credible than psychedelic. It refers to so-called mind-altering substances. Peyote. Cannabis. Ayahuasca. That sort of thing.

There's nothing wrong with entheogens. (Well, except for the occasional severe nausea, vomiting, diarrhea, and so forth.) It's just that they have nothing to do with the simplicity of being. So using entheogens to discover the simplicity of being is a rather ineffective strategy.

Entheogens can, under the right circumstances, provide a powerful means to alter perspective and explore beliefs. Which can be relatively liberating. Nothing wrong with that.

But it's nothing to do with the simplicity of being.

Entheogens can also layer on more concepts and more belief. Nothing wrong with that.

Sometimes those beliefs are more, what you might call, life-affirming. Which is nice.

Sometimes those beliefs are a bit crazy. Which can be stressful.

But in any case, it's nothing to do with the simplicity of being.

I remember reading in Ram Dass' classic, *Be Here Now*, about how he had given LSD to his guru, Neem Karoli Baba. And I was baffled by what Ram Dass reported (in two sources: *Be Here Now* and a later report from another source).

He claimed that on two separate occasions Neem Karoli Baba had requested the "yogi medicine." And on both occasions after taking substantial amounts of the drug he showed no effects.

This story, of course, means nothing. It isn't the truth. It isn't about anything.

Yet it puzzled me. Because I was trying to figure it out. I was trying to understand what "spiritual enlightenment" was.

I had had several LSD trips by that point, and it sort of blew my mind that there was at least an implication that perhaps, just perhaps, the psychedelic experience wasn't it. Because it sure seemed like it might be.

I had mystical experiences with LSD and with psilocybin. I had mystical experiences with mescaline and cannabis.

I can attest that mystical experiences have nothing to do with the simplicity of being.

I had mystical experiences with the Fly Agaric. That was something else entirely. A whole other realm of mysticism.

That was a realm of complete and utter stillness and spaciousness. (Intermixed with periods of complete lunacy. Literally, in my case. I was chasing the moon.)

And I can attest that even the mystical experiences of the Fly Agaric with realms of complete and utter stillness - even with the total clarity of the totality of what is - has nothing to do with the simplicity of being.

(By the way: I cannot in any way advocate for the ingestion of the Fly Agaric - Amanita Muscaria - by anyone who isn't willing to risk a descent into hell from which one may never return. The highs are higher than high. And the rest is sheer madness. And yes, I decarboxylated the mushrooms beforehand.)

To be clear, when I say that things have nothing to do with the simplicity of being, I'm merely stating that these things - whether objects or experiences or states or whatever - are not ways to attain the simplicity of being. They do not lead to the simplicity of being. And the reason for this is hopefully obvious by now: the simplicity of being is all that is. It is already what is. You cannot attain it. This is it.

High or low. Contracted or expanded. Pleasant or unpleasant. Makes no difference.

This is it.

You want high, expanded, pleasant. Orgasmic. Constant. Always more.

Which isn't possible. Or, perhaps it is. And if you want it, keep seeking for it.

But it has nothing whatsoever to do with the simplicity of being. True freedom.

Because. Once again. This is already it. Nothing can give it to you. Nothing can increase it. All of the high, expanded, pleasant, orgasmic, constant as well as the low, contracted, unpleasant is already it.

And when you see this, then you realize that none of it is about you. It isn't yours. It isn't happening to you. You aren't doing it.

There is only this.

If you've had an experience with entheogens then recall an experience right now.

If you haven't had an experience with entheogens then recall any expanded experience that you enjoyed. That felt like it might be "it."

Notice that whatever the content of the experience, there is the simple, direct experiencing. That which is before thought or concept. It is even before sensation. It is even before experience (which is a concept). It is the simple, ordinary sense of existence.

Now notice that right now, as you read this, there is a simple, ordinary sense of existence.

Is there a difference between the simple ordinary sense of existence between these two so-called moments? Or is it the same?

POSITIVE CHANGES

Things are always changing. This is obvious. And worth pointing out.

We all recognize that things are always changing. And we wish for only positive change.

But the reality is that shit happens.

I mean, I'd sure like to always feel healthier and healthier and get more and more wealth and security. It sounds nice.

But it isn't likely to happen.

And if we tell the truth, then isn't much of what passes for "spirituality" really meant to be a sort of insurance policy that more or less guarantees always positive change?

Isn't that the promise of meditation and yoga and qi gong and pranayama and kriya and kundalini practices and prayer and all the rest of it?

This isn't something we normally want to look at too closely.

Still. Take a look.

Look closely. And see that all the pursuit of enlightenment and heaven and nirvana and satori and samadhi and all the rest of it is meant to keep things always on an upward trajectory.

And then see that it's just a huge distraction. Which is fine. There's no problem with distraction.

But it's a set up for suffering.

Change is always happening. And strictly positive, upward, expansive, happy, growth change isn't the only sort of change that happens.

Upon seeing this, the seeker usually sets out trying to escape change.

"If it's not possible to get only positive change, then I'll escape change altogether. I'll escape into the absolute. The changeless source of all that is."

Which is just more of the same. Because the belief is that escaping to the absolute, changeless source is possible for someone.

But it's not.

Because the changeless absolute is not one, not two.

And it's already what is.

There is no one already. Take a look.

Where is the one who wants only positive change? Where is the one who wants to escape into changeless source?

Where is the thinker? Where is the observer? Where is the seer? Where is the one you call yourself?

I remember that once upon a time I had reasoned the whole thing out. I had figured, quite reasonably, that if everything is changing (which is quite apparently the case) then the only way that this could be seen is from a point that, at least relative to itself, is still.

This was my attempt to escape.

There is no escape. Give up the attempts to escape.

After I had reasoned out my escape, I suffered for at least another five years.

And what ended the suffering wasn't finally escaping to the changeless source.

What ended suffering was the clear seeing that there is only ever this. There isn't anything apart from this. There is no escape. There is no separate individual. There is no point of stillness. There is no changeless source.

There is only this.

And you can call this changeless source. Because that's as good a name as any. But it's not that. It's this. All names are lies. Even the best of them. Even capitalized names like Source or Spirit or Consciousness or God or Brahman.

There is only this. And this is evident right now when you simply look.

Right now, notice that in direct experience, before names and labels and memories and ideas, there is only this. You cannot put a name to this. Nor can you capture it in thought.

There is no moment. There is no now. There is no here. There is no thing.

And yet, there is this. Undeniable. Unavoidable.

Right now. Look. Feel. Be. Can you find change? Can you find changelessness? Can you find anything?

There is only this. Neither changing nor changeless. All

apparent change is this present arising. All apparent changelessness is this present arising.

And notice that this is not happening to you. Nor is it about you. There is no you. There is only this.

POSITIVE THINKING

Pointing out the utter futility and pointlessness of so-called positive thinking is one of my special joys. Perhaps because I fell prey to the insidious disease of positive thinking for many years.

We live in a positive thinking culture. Not, of course, that there's a lot of positive thinking going on. Rather, the culture tends to promote the idea of positive thinking as something desirable.

So it's not a surprise that so many of us have gotten sucked into the positive thinking trap.

I know that I've said this many times before. So at the risk of beating a dead horse (what an image!) I'll say it again: thought is just thought. It's meaningless. It is powerless. It's just thought.

The trap of positive thinking is that it can seem as though there's someone choosing the thoughts. And then that only reinforces the painful mistaken identity as the chooser of the thoughts.

Upon awakening to the simplicity of being it is evident that thought is merely thought. And all evaluation of thought as good or bad becomes entirely silly. It becomes clear that it's just not worth giving much attention to thought. (Not that there's anyone to choose that, either!)

Really, does it matter if you think the thought "I'm a winner" or "I'm a loser?"

It only seems to matter because there's another thought that says it matters. And you are fixated on thought. As if thought was real. As if thought referenced something.

Take a look right now. Where do thoughts come from? Who chooses the thoughts? What are thoughts made out of? What are the qualities of thought? Can you hold a thought? Can you touch a thought? Can you see a thought? Can you taste a thought? Can you smell a thought?

Think a thought. Go ahead. It's alright. And if you want a particular thought to think, then here it is: bread.

Now, as you think of bread, notice does the thought bread taste like bread? Does it smell like bread? Does it feel like bread? Can the thought satisfy your hunger?

Does the thought 'bread' actually reference bread? Or is it merely a thought? It *seems* to reference something, but only because you assumed as much.

So go ahead and take a closer look. Examine the assumptions. Does the thought reference anything?

Does thought have any substance at all? Is there anything there?

There is no chooser of thought. And thought has no substance. Nor does it reference anything of substance. There is nothing there.

Pretty cool, huh?

I suffered tremendously from thought for a very long time. I was severely obsessive. And so thought was a major problem for me.

So you can imagine what a relief it was to discover that there is no thought and no me. Whew!

But don't take my word for it. Look for yourself.

Don't try to see no thought and no me. That won't work.

Instead, just examine the assumptions. You assume there is thought and you assume there is a me. But notice that you look to thought to prove the existence of thought and the existence of me. You want to reason it out.

Don't.

Just look to direct experience. Look right now. Feel right now. Notice if you can find anything. Can you find a thought? Can you find a me?

BEING MORE PRESENT, MORE NOW

Ever since the *Power of Now* was published I can't even tell you how many conversations I've had in which people want to be more present. They want to be more now.

I know this may be hard to believe. But I've got to break the news to you.

There is no now.

You can't get more present. Because there is no you and there is no present.

And don't think that I'm just mincing words. I'm not. Take a look for yourself. Right now.

Can you find now? Can you find the present? Can you find you?

Don't look to thought. Thought is only thought. It cannot give you anything other than thought.

So instead, look only to direct experience. Feel only what is immediate. Sense what is direct.

Can you find now? Or is there only this?

When I say this, I don't mean anything by it. I'm not talking about a special this. I'm talking about this. This right now. Exactly as it is. This. Whatever it is.

Is this now? Or is it just this?

Can you find the present? Or is there only this?

Can you find you? Or is there only this?

Where else are you going to go? Then? There?

The usual answer is thought. People think that they are going to thought and therefore escaping now or not being present.

Where is thought? Can you find thought? Find a thought. Go ahead. Do it. Right now. Can you find it?

Be careful. Don't settle for a thought as an answer. Really find a thought. Grab ahold of it. Feel it. Take in the qualities and attributes of it. Notice the texture, the smell, the taste of the thought. Can you locate a thought?

There is no thought. Thought is only a fiction. It's a mirage.

I'm not suggesting that thought doesn't appear to happen. It does. But upon closer examination can you actually find a thought?

Just as a mirage on a road always remains out of reach. Just as you can never reach the end of a rainbow. Thought is an illusion.

There is nothing other than this. You cannot be other than this. There is no you. No now. No present. No thing.

No time. No space. Just this.

As always. Don't take my word for it. See for yourself. Can you find anything?

BEING TOO IN THE MIND

Have you ever had the experience of being caught up in your mind?

Now. Examine this experience of being caught up in your mind. What are the qualities of this experience?

Look to your own experience for the answers.

Whatever qualities you find are what you find. There is no right answer.

Now, if you take away each of those qualities, what remains?

In other words, if the experience has no qualities, then what is it?

Is there an experience independent of the qualities?

Notice how we give names to experiences and then we think that the experiences have some sort of independent existence.

But they don't. There is no experience apart from the

qualities of the experience.

Let's take another example. Eating an apple.

What are the qualities? Obviously every apple is different. But for this example I'll suggest the following qualities. Sweet. Tart. Crunchy. Juicy. Cool.

Take away the qualities, and what is left? Can you eat an apple without any qualities? Without the qualities there is no experience.

The qualities are the experience. There is no such thing as an experience.

Can you see that the experience of being caught up in your mind is merely a collection of qualities to which you have given a name and meaning? But the experience is a fiction.

There is no mind. Can you find it? Where is it? What is its shape? Its color? Its size?

And once again, can you find you?

There is no you to be caught up in the mind. There is no mind to be caught up in.

All there is, is this. And it can seem to have qualities. Yet even the qualities, upon closer inspection, turn out to be simply this.

There is nothing apart from this. You cannot understand this. This is all there is.

NEEDING TIME (TO SET ASIDE TIME)

There is a persistent myth that in order to awaken to the simplicity of being you must dedicate yourself to years or lifetimes of dedicated practice. In other words, you need a lot of time.

Strangely, I hear people defending this position with great tenacity. In fact, many people seem to get upset at the mere suggestion that it doesn't require so much time and effort.

Actually, it requires absolutely no time and absolutely no effort. And any time and any effort are merely putting off clear seeing of what is as it is. It's that simple.

All time is more delusion. All time is more putting off what is unavoidable.

Upon awakening to the simplicity of being (which happens right now) it is obvious that there is only this ever-present happening. There is no before. There is no after.

There is no now. There is just this.

How can more time get you to what you never left? What you cannot leave? What is already the case?

This is it. This right now.

Notice how you have ideas about what the simplicity of being is and what awakening to the simplicity of being will be like. And yet all you have to do is see how these ideas are absolutely meaningless. There is nothing other than this. So give up your idea that there is something else. This already is the simplicity of being.

SHADOW

Some teachers whose work I respect suggest that even after awakening to the simplicity of being, one continues to have a "shadow". And then these teachers go on to suggest that one who has awakened to the simplicity of being is best to do what they call "shadow work".

I may retract my statements in regard to this some months or years from now. But honest to goodness, I can find absolutely none of this shadow business in my own experience.

The reason is that I cannot find anyone or anything, much less a shadow.

I have had enough conversations about this subject now, however, that I am beginning to suspect that those who advocate for shadow work are pointing to a more complex simplicity of being than I am.

Because in the simplicity of being there is only this.

And "only this" is not an excuse to "misbehave" or act "badly".

Rather, in my experience, this is an endless, ever-present "meeting" of all that is. There is no chooser. There is no separate self. There is no motivation to lie or cheat or steal or "misbehave".

Now, none of that is to say that the behavior of the apparent individual will necessarily conform to everyone's expectations. Because it won't.

Let's face it. No behavior conforms to everyone's expectations.

It's just that in the apparent individual who sees all exactly as it is rather than as it is imagined to be, there is not so much inner conflict that motivates so much of the behavior that we normally see.

And, of course, all of that is completely not true. Because there is no individual. No thing. Only this.

The common way in which people get hung up on this is that they then get caught up in thoughts such as the infamous "but then won't people just turn into murderers and thieves and abusers of all sorts?"

Which, in my view, is a complete misunderstanding of what I am pointing to. The whole idea that seeing what is as it is will somehow result in more violent and criminal behavior is ridiculous. It presupposes that there is a separate individual who will cross some finish line and then get a "get out of jail free" card for life that will excuse all sorts of horrific behavior.

But that's not what I'm pointing to.

I'm not pointing to any sort of individual. I'm not pointing to any sort of arrival. I'm not pointing to any*thing*.

There is only ever this. Seeing this clearly doesn't liberate any individual. It doesn't fundamentally change anything. It simply reveals what is, as it is. Which is what is already the case.

And, strangely, from my own experience and observation, clear seeing tends to actually produce *less* violence rather than more. It tends to produce greater compassion and peace. This isn't something that anyone does. It is not the result of "working on" one's self. It isn't because there is anyone striving to be more compassionate and peaceful.

It's just that strangely, once it is obvious that there is no one separate from this, then the seeming inner conflict and stress and fear just can't be believed any longer.

EGO

There are two men who have reinforced the nonsensical concept of ego in modern popular culture: Ram Dass and Eckhart Tolle. And because these two men are so revered, it seems that most people will continue to believe in ego for some time now.

You don't have to be most people.

So I'll let you in on a secret: there is no ego.

Go ahead and find it. Can you? Look to direct experience and find the ego.

Ego is to spirit as the Dark Side is to the Light Side in the Star Wars universe. But can you see that ego and spirit are just as fictional as Star Wars? It's a nice story. But that's all.

There is no Luke Skywalker. There is no Darth Vader. There is no ego. There is no spirit. There is only this.

This is not a thing. This is not nothing either. Because then nothing gets turned into a subtle thing.

Ego is the evil against which we are taught to fight in order to gain liberation.

But notice how when I remove ego in one fell swoop there is a sense of resistance that can arise.

If ego is bad and getting rid of ego is desirable, then my announcement that there is no ego should bring elation.

The trouble is that there is no spirit either. And this feels like a letdown. This feels like a disappointment.

Can you see how the myth of ego is needed to reinforce the myth of spirit? The myth of the Dark Side is needed to prop up the myth of the Light Side.

There is nothing wrong with myth. There is nothing wrong with fiction. There is nothing wrong with fantasy.

It's just that it has nothing to do with the simplicity of being.

The simplicity of being is already this. What you call ego is the simplicity of being. What you call spirit is the simplicity of being. Neither exists. There is only this.

There is a non-existent coin. One side is ego. The other side is spirit. You want spirit without ego. This is an impossibility on two counts. For one thing, you cannot have a one-sided coin. And for another, the coin is non-existent.

There is only this. Ego is not a problem. Spirit is not attainable. Because there is only this. There is nothing apart from this. This is non-conceptual.

STILL FEELING SEPARATE/NOT FEELING ONENESS

How will you know when you've arrived? How will you know when you are finally enlightened?

I knew how I was going to know: I was going to *feel* it.

I wasn't quite sure what it would feel like. I just knew that this wasn't it.

If you pressed me, then I'd probably admit that I expected that spiritual enlightenment would feel like the effects of MDMA (the drug more commonly known as Ecstasy). MDMA feels really good. At least for the first four to eight hours. After that, it feels awful.

I wanted just the first bit. The really good feelings. That's what I imagined awakening to the simplicity of being would be like.

And, I suppose, that it *does* feel like that. That is, for the first four-eight hours after one takes MDMA.

And then it feels like whatever it feels like.

Right now it feels like this.

Notice how in some way you have a concept of what awakening to the simplicity of being will be like. Notice how you have to reference some past experience. Maybe a drug experience. Or a meditation experience. Or a sexual experience. Or a purely spontaneous experience.

You probably imagine that it feels expanded, peaceful, happy, and joyful.

What are those feelings? Notice that when you look more closely what you are actually wanting are specific physical sensations.

Right now notice that there are physical sensations in your body. And see how you subtly compare these sensations to the sensations that you believe are the sensations of awakening in order to judge that this isn't it.

That's all that is going on. It's just a comparison of present experience with some arbitrary concept of what you imagine would be better.

That's all.

In reality, this is it. This is all that is. There is nothing apart from this. And this is exactly what the simplicity of being feels like. This. Exactly this.

In reality the only thing that seemingly obscures the clear seeing of this as it is already, is the idea that there is something else that *could* be. As if there is some other experience possible.

This is it.

This is not a thought. Not a concept. This is reality. This is truth. Look to direct experience right now and what else can you find?

Can you see that even the concept that there is something else that might happen that will be called spiritual enlightenment or spiritual awakening or anything else is merely this present arising?

If you believe that you haven't arrived yet because you don't yet feel oneness, then just look to see what oneness feels like. And then notice where that idea exists. Can you find the idea in direct experience?

Remain with direct experience. Is there anything else? Can you find anything apart from this? This is what reality feels like. Exactly this. And now this. And now this. Always this.

CHOICE/CHOICELESSNESS

I used to get tied up in mental knots trying to sort out the whole mess of "if there is no separate self then how can there be choice?"

And really, it's just a waste of time. Because once it is evident that there is only this then it is also evident that all is uncaused. So there is no longer any need to try and puzzle out the choice/choicelessness riddle. It collapses into the totality of this ever-present reality.

But until then, I find that it is best to simply give up on trying to puzzle out the mess. You won't figure it out. It's just an endless distraction.

Instead, just assume that there is choice. But don't get caught up in trying to figure that out either. Don't worry about "big" choices. In fact, there is only one choice that you should ever make.

And that choice is to remain with direct experience and

try and find anything other than this.

In *I Am That*, Nisargadatta Maharaj reported: "I trusted my Guru. What he told me to do, I did. He told me to concentrate on 'I am' - I did. He told me that I am beyond all perceivables and conceivables - I believed."

The more that I consider this statement, the more wise it seems to me.

If only we can hear and trust this good advice, then we can be free of the delusion of separation and complication. Remain with direct experience. Try and find something other than this.

And when you cannot, then you see what is, as it is. Then you cease to believe in anything else. You become very simple. Utterly simple. The simplicity of being.

TRYING TO FIND "I" OR SELF

A lot of the popular contemporary Western non-duality teachings of which I am aware are influenced greatly by the teachings of Ramana Maharshi and Nisargadatta Maharaj. And oftentimes the instructions of these men speak of focusing on "I" or they will speak of residing in the self. In fact, self is often capitalized: Self. And this all gives the wrong impression that there is something to find.

Although from here the instructions are clear, because there is no longer any confusion or seeking. And that makes things rather inherently clear.

Yet for my part, when I was seeking, these sorts of instructions and the references to Self, and self-realization, and residing in the Self left me very confused. And I was seeking for something. I was seeking for something called

Self.

The trouble is that there is no Self. There is no "I." There is no thing.

There is only this. And this is not a thing.

So while the instructions given from these traditions can be very useful and practical, they can also be misleading.

Don't look for a nothing called "Self". Don't look for a nothing called "I am". Just remain with direct experience. Stay here. And see if you can find anything. Including what you imagine to be yourself. Including what you imagine to be Self. See if you can find anything.

In other words, the mistake that I made and the mistake that I often see other people making is to look for *nothing*. This is often a problem because the implication is that there is someone looking for nothing. But instead, look at the assumptions of anything that is separate or individual. Look for *things*. Examine them closely until you recognize what is without resorting to thought to give you an answer.

DANGER THOUGHTS

I used to be severely anxious. For several years I was in a constant state of panic. I couldn't sleep but a few hours a day. I was constantly on guard. And I was paranoid.

I saw danger at every turn. I was anticipating danger. Everything that I did was dangerous. Even eating or drinking water (*especially* eating and drinking water) felt horrifically dangerous.

So I know a thing or two about thoughts of danger. My experiences were so extreme that it eventually gave me a rather unique perspective. From here it is evident that *all* thoughts about danger are merely thoughts.

This is often one of the most difficult things for people to see. Because feelings of danger are so primal. And so people often give undue attention to thoughts of danger.

In fact, feelings of danger completely subvert rationality.

Feelings of danger originate in the primitive parts of the brain that simply react.

There is nothing wrong with feelings of danger. Feelings of danger are not a problem in the least. Feelings of danger are not opposed to the simplicity of being. The simplicity of being is always this.

The only trouble is that when you attach meaning to the feelings and you pursue efforts to find solutions, your attention fixates on thought. And this can be very, very unpleasant. And, it can *seem* to obscure the simplicity of being.

To be clear, none of this matters one iota to the simplicity of being. The simplicity of being is regardless of danger or not, regardless of danger thoughts or not . . . regardless of anything.

Still, danger thoughts can preoccupy one's mind, seeming to obscure the clarity of the simplicity of being.

The thing that finally changed this vicious cycle of danger obsession for me was recognizing that thoughts are not helpful in dealing with danger. So any thoughts about danger are useless and can be immediately discarded.

Thoughts about danger can spin out of control into a giant mess of anxiety pretty quickly. "I smell something strange" can lead to "it might be a toxin" can lead to "where is it coming from?" can lead to "it's coming from the neighboring apartment" can lead to "my neighbor is spraying pesticides" can lead to "I have to get out of here" and on and on.

From a calm perspective these thoughts aren't particularly

believable. But after you've started believing the thoughts, then no matter how crazy the story spins it all seems real. The danger can seem very real.

In fact, you feel it just as if there really was an imminent threat.

And while none of this has anything to do with the simplicity of being, it can seem to obscure the simplicity of being. It doesn't actually obscure the simplicity of being. Because this is always the simplicity of being.

But it can seem to obscure the simplicity of being.

So my advice is that you simply discard all danger thoughts. Don't get rid of them. Because you cannot. But just let them go.

Keep your attention with the direct experience.

And when you do this, you will likely notice some intense physical sensations. Some of which you may label as unpleasant.

Let go of the thoughts that tell you to get rid of the sensations or change the sensations. Don't try to change the sensations.

Just remain with the direct experience. Insist on direct, unmediated experience. Do not settle for a thought or a name or a label or a concept.

"Unpleasant" is a label. "Unwanted" is a label. "Tense" is a label. "Adrenaline" is a label. "Stress" is a label. "Fear" is a label.

Refuse to settle for a label. Just stay with direct, unmediated experience.

Even "sensation" is a label.

Notice that as you remain with direct experience, the experience changes. So there never was a thing you could label. The second you label it, it's not that. It never was that.

It is always this. Just remain with this.

And when danger thoughts vie for your attention, just remain with this. Trust that there is nothing that is more important than this.

If any action is necessary, it will be obvious. It will not require thought. Just remain with this.

Direct. Unmediated. This.

My hope is that you can simply trust me. I have been through the wringer. I had *lots* of danger thoughts. You name it, I've probably thought it. And believed it.

And I assure you that it is not necessary. Nor is it helpful. And giving attention to the danger thoughts only serves to *seemingly* obscure the simplicity of being.

It doesn't obscure the simplicity of being. Because even this is the simplicity of being. Whatever this is. Whatever happens. This is always the simplicity of being. Nothing can obscure that.

But giving attention to danger thoughts seems to affirm the existence of someone separate. Which is observably false. So stay with direct experience. And know what is real. This is the only way that ever worked for me. It is the only way that I have ever seen work for others.

STABILIZATION

Stabilization is a myth. There is no stabilization. There is only this.

Stabilization implies that there is something else. There is not. There is only this.

So if you feel that you have only to "stabilize" then you are deluding yourself.

What will you stabilize in? Who will stabilize in it? Where will the stabilization occur? And when will it occur?

Look to direct experience right now. Can you find anyone? Can you find anything? Can you find anywhere? Can you find any time?

Stabilization is a concept. It is another thought. It is a thought that seems to remember one type of experience that it labels as "desirable". And it then compares that memory with what it thinks of the present experience - which it labels as "not enough."

Then thought suggests that "you" need to "stabilize" in that desirable state.

It's a lie.

Again, look to direct experience. Right now, can you find you? Can you find another state? Can you find any state?

Or is there simply this?

NO MORE FEAR

One of the ways in which people often believe that they will know when they have finally become spiritually enlightened (whatever that means) is that they will no longer experience fear or regret or guilt or shame or any of those "unspiritual" emotions.

And then, of course, they start to monitor to see if they are still feeling fear, regret, or any of the unspiritual emotions.

Which they are.

So they aren't yet enlightened.

This is so complicated and completely useless.

Awakening to the simplicity of being has nothing to do with fear, regret, guilt, shame, or any other emotional state.

The simplicity of being includes everything. This right now is the simplicity of being. Including the appearance of what you call unspiritual emotions. Including the appearance of what you call yourself. Including hate crime. Including murders. Including wars. Including everything.

The only problem is that you make a useless distinction between various experiences, and you imagine that some are spiritual while others are unspiritual. Some are good while others are bad. You want to keep some and get rid of others.

Take a look right now and see if you can find an emotion.

Can you find anything apart from this?

Feeling what seems to be particular emotions has nothing to do with anything. It is just this. It is only this. There is nothing apart from this.

Don't take my word for it. Just look for yourself. Can you find anything else?

And if you cannot find anything else apart from this in direct experience then can you see that all experience is merely this? Not as a concept. Not as a belief. Just as immediate, direct experience right now.

There is no measure of whether you are enlightened or not. Because you will never be enlightened. What you conceive of as you is merely the seeking for something else. The moment that you remain with direct experience then you cease to exist as something separate. Or, rather, it is obvious that there is only this and nothing apart from this.

"SPIRITUAL" EXPERIENCE

Nearly every spiritual seeker has a story of her or his first major "spiritual" experience.

Looking from here the funny thing is that all experience gets leveled, and the idea of any experience being more "spiritual" than another or more important than another is completely transparent. There is no such thing as a "spiritual" experience. There is only this.

Nonetheless, as far as the story goes, my first major "spiritual" experience happened while listening to a Ken Cohen Qi Gong meditation cassette tape that my friend, Leo, had loaned to me.

I was 19 years old, and living on my own in a new city. Leo was a new friend. We had struck a friendship in large part because we both expressed a keen interest in exploring the nature of reality.

I burned some white sage, and then I sat down on my bed

and listened to the tape through headphones. The meditation was a guided set of breathing exercises culminating in what is called embryonic breath.

At that point in the meditation I believe that Ken Cohen describes a golden egg. In that moment my sense of self rapidly expanded and dissolved like a big bang of consciousness. And for the next timeless moment I had no sense of myself in the ordinary sense. I was aware. Much like deep sleep. Except subtly seeming to be more conscious. Whatever that means.

I've had other people report their major spiritual experiences to me. Sometimes they last seconds. Sometimes hours. Sometimes days. Sometimes even months.

And then they end.

So-called "spiritual" experiences are really just delightful, pleasant, expanded, subtle types of experiences. They can be wonderful.

But these experiences have nothing to do with the simplicity of being.

Much like psychedelic experiences, these "spiritual" experiences can lead one to pursue more, more, more.

There's nothing wrong with that. But it's nothing to do with the simplicity of being.

The simplicity of being is what is regardless of experience - "spiritual" or otherwise.

The simplicity of being is completely unaffected by any experience.

Spiritual experience is no better than any other experience. It just *seems* that way to you. That's because you assign value and meaning and then believe it. That's all.

The idea that spiritual experience isn't so important can be hard to swallow for some people. For me it became easier and easier to accept because eventually everything in my life became flat and low. I became deeply and thoroughly depressed.

Even copious amounts of extremely potent cannabis failed to produce so much as a little boost in mood. I felt no joy. No elation. No expansion. Just depressed.

So eventually, I was ripe, as they say.

You don't have to wait for this sort of thing, though. Just stay with direct experience. Just tell the truth. Just be radically honest. Refuse to accept any thoughts or labels or concepts as answers.

Refuse to accept any answers. Just remain with what is, as it is. Direct. Immediate. Unavoidable.

And see for yourself that spiritual experience is essentially meaningless. It's not even a taste of true awakening to the simplicity of being. Because it's just another state. Just another experience.

And the simplicity of being is all that is.

ALMOST THERE

I remember going on long road trips during the summer as a child. I would watch the mirage out ahead on the hot roadway. It appeared that just up ahead there was a pool of water on the road.

And yet, we never reached it. No matter how far we drove, the water was always out ahead.

The pursuit of awakening to the simplicity of being can be like that.

There's a word for this sort of thing. That word is compulsion.

You are not almost there. You will never be any closer. You cannot get there.

What you are doing is not working. It will never work. You will not become spiritually enlightened. You will not awaken to the simplicity of being.

It's a mirage. And it keeps you going.

Like a dehydrated man in the desert pursuing water just ahead, you keep going and you prolong your suffering.

Awakening to the simplicity of being is not an event that happens in time. It is the collapsing of the belief in time. It is the collapsing of the belief in space. It is the collapsing of the belief in a separate you.

None of that means that anything will be different "after" awakening. It won't. Because this is already it. It will be exactly like this.

Upon recognizing that the mirage of water is just a mirage that will always appear to be just ahead this doesn't end the mirage. And in the same way, even though the belief in time, space, and a separate me is no longer doesn't mean that I now perceive anything differently than before. It is exactly the same. Because it always has been just this. There is nothing else.

Right now, take a look and see if you can find this destination to which you are so close to arriving. Can you find it? Is it really there?

Can you find anything apart from this? Is there any separate person to arrive somewhere or attain something?

LIVING TEACHER

Finding the right teacher used to be a big deal for me. I felt a "resonance," as they say in non-duality circles, with Papaji. But Papaji had died five years before I learned of him.

Did I need a living teacher? So many teachers spoke of this need to have a living teacher. So I set out to find the "right" living teacher.

I went from teacher to teacher, satsang to satsang, in my search for "the one." I imagined that upon meeting "the one" that I would know somehow. Perhaps my heart would burst into flame. Or my mind would go blank. Or my sense of self would expand into infinity.

I never met the teacher that had this effect on me. So the doubt always remained.

Finally, upon seeing clearly the reality of what is as it is, the whole idea of needing a "living teacher" in the form of another person seems completely laughable.

It's just another thing to get hung up on. There is no need for a teacher at all. Because no one can give you what already is. No one can transmit some special spiritual energy that will end your search. It's a fantasy. And why so many teachers perpetuate this fantasy is a mystery.

Sure, having someone who can point you clearly to what is unavoidable is helpful. And we're all different, so what works for one won't necessarily work for everyone. So if you can find the "right" teacher for you, that is certainly "nice to have."

But it's not necessary.

All that is necessary is that you remain with direct experience. Just stay here. That is all.

If you do this, then nothing else is necessary. And even if you work one-on-one with all the "greatest" spiritual teachers then it will be of no use to you if you don't remain with direct experience.

Really. Truly. Honestly. It's *so much simpler* than you think it is. You don't need more teachings. You don't need more teachers. You don't need a living teacher. You don't need an enlightened master. Just remain with direct experience. Just see clearly for yourself. Just refuse to accept any answer for anything.

That is all.

DIET

So many teachers perpetuate the myth of the role of diet in awakening to the simplicity of being. And this is a huge disservice to seekers. Because diet has absolutely nothing to do with awakening to the simplicity of being. Nothing. Not in the least.

Vegetarianism is not more spiritual than eating meat. Sattvic diets are not more conducive to awakening to reality as it is than eating lots of garlic, potatoes, and hamburgers. Green tea isn't better for your spiritual well-being than Mountain Dew. (Though it's probably better for your liver!) And shopping at your local, organic farmers' market doesn't give you more spiritual points than McDonald's.

I know this can be hard to believe. Because you want to believe that you can earn spiritual enlightenment. But there is no such thing. There is no thing at all. All these concepts are just concepts.

My suggestion is that you stop trying so hard to make anything mean anything. Because nothing means anything. It's all completely meaningless.

Eat what you want to eat. Eat what tastes good. Eat what satisfies your hunger. Eat what feels good to eat. And let go. Because none of it means anything. Really. Honestly. Truly.

Food is just food. Eating is just eating. And reality is reality no matter what.

If what you eat could possibly have anything to do with the truth of what is as it is then that would have to make you someone separate. You'd have to be a separate individual with volition. So look right now and see if you can find a separate individual who can get closer to or further from something else called awakening.

Can you find anything separate from this present happening when you look to direct experience?

Can you see how so much of the seeming problem is merely unexamined assumption?

INTELLECTUAL UNDERSTANDING

Perhaps one of the most common questions that I hear seekers asking (and one that I asked often enough) is how it is possible that they have an "intellectual understanding" of the simplicity of being and yet they still suffer. They want to know what more they need to do or how they can understand the simplicity of being "perfectly."

The trouble is that an intellectual understanding has absolutely nothing whatsoever to do with the simplicity of being. Furthermore, you absolutely cannot understand the simplicity of being. By definition, if you can understand it, then what you understand is not the simplicity of being.

The simplicity of being is so utterly simple and immediate that there is absolutely no possibility of understanding it. Really. I kid you not. I'm 100% serious about this. You cannot understand this. You will never understand this. It is impossible. And if you understand something then you misunderstand entirely what I am pointing to.

I used to be caught up in the vicious cycle of "intellectual understanding". It's useless. Truly. It will never give you what you most want.

Because what you most want is what is already the case. What you most want is the total and complete freedom of what is. And all so-called understanding is merely arising in and as this total freedom. No understanding can ever give you this.

The simplest, easiest way to awaken to the simplicity of being of which I am aware is to trace every impulse to understand back to its source. Discover where it comes from. Discover what it is.

This is exactly the same as remaining with direct experience. It is exactly the same as refusing to accept any answer. It is exactly the same as effortless being. There truly is no effort involved. It is not a doing. It is not an attainment. It is just this. This is unavoidable. Just this.

I DON'T LIVE IT YET

Another take on the same old story is the notion that you aren't yet living awakening. The implication here is that you either understand it (which hopefully now you see as a fantasy) or you have glimpsed it in the past, and now you are trying to get back to it.

Or, there is the third option, which is that you fantasize about something that you haven't ever actually experienced and that you don't understand, but you believe that there is some future state that you might attain that will be better than this.

In any one of these cases, the reality remains exactly this present happening. And regardless of your thoughts or beliefs or memories or ambitions, this remains all that is. There will never be anything other than this.

In direct experience, refusing to accept any answers, can

you find anything apart from this? Can you see that all the notions about becoming enlightened or awakening to something are merely conceptual fantasies arising in this present happening?

Can you see that the whole idea of something else is complicated? Yet what is, is utterly simple. There is only this. It is utterly simple. Don't complicate it. Don't go anywhere else. There is nowhere else to go anyway! Just remain here. Direct. Immediate. This.

STOP THOUGHTS

I address the misconception of a silent mind over and over because it is one of the most persistent myths that serves as an obstacle for seekers.

Some very influential teachers over the years have suggested that one who is awakened to the simplicity of being has a silent mind. They will even sometimes go so far as to state that they have no thoughts.

This is misleading on several accounts. For one thing, there is no one who awakens. There is only the simplicity of being. So upon seeing reality as it is there is no longer the delusion of an individual having a separate mind that could be relatively more or less silent than anything else. Rather, there is only this.

The second thing that is misleading about these statements is that they at least leave open the implication that it is possible or desirable to stop thoughts or silence thoughts.

And in my experience this is a complete impossibility. Well, other than brain damage. But I overdo that joke.

Go ahead. Try to stop your thoughts. Don't think a thought for 20 seconds. Or even just ten seconds. Or even just five seconds.

If you try not to think a thought then you become aware that there is no one thinking the thoughts. Thoughts merely appear. You don't choose them. There is no you to choose them.

Yet a curious thing happens when you remain with direct experience. Absolutely nothing changes. You don't do anything about anything. You don't change thoughts or get rid of thoughts or do anything with thoughts. And somehow, thoughts disappear. Or, rather, it becomes obvious that thoughts don't exist. There are no thoughts.

So the irony is that the harder you try to get rid of thoughts, the more the thoughts seem to get reinforced. Yet when you cease to look to thoughts to give you any answers, thoughts reveal their true nature - which is that they are non-existent.

Thoughts are not a problem. Give no attention to them. Simply stay with what is unavoidable.

BEING THE OBSERVER

Many "mindfulness" practices involve witnessing and observing. And I have heard plenty of reports from people in which they tell of how they now witness everything that they do.

Which is fine.

But it has absolutely nothing to do with the simplicity of being.

The whole act of observing or witnessing creates another identity. Now, instead of imagining that you are this person named Jim or Jane, you're the witness. You're the silence. You're the spaciousness. You're the doing. You're the happening. You're the experiencing.

And none of that is actually true.

Because in direct experience it is impossible to find any of that. Just look right now. See if you can find anyone. Even a subtle someone. See if you can find the witness. See if you can find the observer.

Notice how the sense of being the witness or the observer is yet another experience. It is another state. It is something to recreate and grab ahold of and maintain.

Which is fine. It's just nothing to do with the simplicity of being.

The simplicity of being is. So. Much. Simpler.

It's utterly simple. It's not a state. It's not about witnessing. It's not about observing.

It's just this. What is before, during, and after all observing and all witnessing. It is what remains as all identities come and go. It is what is always the case. It is unavoidable.

And neither can you observe it nor witness it. There is no room for that. There is no time for that. There is no one to observe and nothing to observe. There is only this.

HAVE TO GET RID OF ILLUSION

One of the trickiest illusions is the illusion of illusion. Because there is no such thing. There is only this. And this is not illusion. This is simply this.

It *appears* that there is illusion. But this is only because of the mistaken sense of being someone separate from what is. Upon seeing this then there is no longer any confusion about it.

Perhaps the best analogy that I can come up with at the moment is that it's a bit like waking from a dream of watching a movie about a mirage. Upon waking what happened to the mirage? Was there ever a mirage? Or is there only this?

When you see it this way then perhaps you can start to see the futility of trying to get rid of the illusion. Because trying to get rid of a non-existent illusion serves no purpose other than to reinforce the fictional sense of an illusion.

There is no problem with illusion. Let it happen. It is uncaused anyway. It's not *your* illusion.

So-called enlightened people (whoever they are) see the illusion for what it is. Which is simply this. There is nothing separate from this. There is only ever this. Which includes the illusion.

And when you remain with reality as it is, refusing to accept an answer to anything, then you see that there never was an illusion. There is only ever this.

This is true freedom.

AFRAID OF DISAPPEARING

Sometimes people get hung up on the fear of disappearing. They get it in their heads that by recognizing their true nature they will simply vanish. As in, everything will cease to exist.

The problem with this sort of thinking is just that it's a concept. It's a fear based on an idea. It's a fantasy.

It's sort of like being afraid of the bogie man.

When I was four years old I became friends with a neighbor girl. One day we were playing, and she told me that she was afraid of the bogie man.

I had never heard of the bogie man. I was curious. After all, if she was afraid of him then I wanted to know at least enough to know how to steer clear of him.

The trouble was that she couldn't really describe him to me. She had never actually seen him.

All she could say was that her father had told her about

the bogie man. And she imagined that he could probably walk through walls.

So I tried really hard to picture the bogie man. I stared at the wall. I screwed up my face and squinted and turned my head sideways.

All I could visualize was her father's face. I didn't find him to be too scary. So I gave up on visualizing the bogie man.

Look to your direct experience. Right now. Can you find a bogie man? Can you find a thought? Can you find San Francisco? Can you find Batman? Can you find LSD? Can you find the Purple Pieman? Can you find anything at all that is separate from this?

By this I mean exactly this. Whatever this is. This that is evident in direct experience. Before thought. Before experience. Just this.

Can you find anything separate? Anything at all?

This is all that I am ever pointing to. Just this. Nothing else.

This is not a concept. This is not something that can disappear. This is not a thing. This is always this. It is completely non-conceptual. Completely free.

This is the totality. This is all that is.

SADNESS ABOUT NO SELF

I have heard people report feeling sadness about the possibility of no self.

I understand. I used to feel sadness when I thought that I caught glimpses of no self.

I felt an emptiness. Not bad. Not loss. Just emptiness.

But it felt sad. It felt lonely.

The trouble was that I was still seeing emptiness as something separate. I still was imagining that I was the seer of emptiness. I was still imagining that emptiness was a thing.

Emptiness is not a thing.

There is no seer.

There is no separation.

There is only this. This is not one, not two.

Emptiness seems empty when seen as a thing. When seen as something separate. When seen by an (imaginary) seer.

Yet emptiness is not a thing. Emptiness is not separate.

There is no seer.

There is only this.

And when this is truly seen as it is, then what appeared to be emptiness is seen to be the totality.

Totality is all that is. Totality is not a thing. To give it any attributes is misleading.

And yet, it would be equally misleading to suggest that it is not also overflowing joy, love, compassion, and happiness.

It's just that you cannot ever understand any of this. The second you try to capture this in thought and turn it into a thing with qualities that you think of as joy, love, compassion, and happiness, then it is none of that.

It is just this.

This is all that is.

Just this.

Exactly this.

Simply this.

GET ANOTHER OF MY BOOKS FOR FREE

I would be delighted to give you yet another of my books (normally priced at $3.99) for free.

Here are some of the things that reviewers have to say about my book *No One Home*:

> "The book is EXCELLENT! Joey found a wonderful way of using words to help you see that what you have been searching for is right here"

> "[The] clearest direct non-duality book I have read"

> "I'm feeling a real wave of gratitude for discovering his clear pointing out instructions"

> "[I]f you relax and enjoy the process with honest curiosity, you will know directly what the buddhas and bodhisattvas have been pointing to all these centuries"

And you can get it for FREE by visiting http://joeylott.com/no-one-home-free-offer

PLEASE WRITE A REVIEW OF THIS BOOK

If you liked this book, it would be fabulous if you would write a review of it on site of the retailer from which you got the book

I know, I know. You think it doesn't matter. And it is sort of obnoxious that I ask you to take a minute from your valuable time to do something like write a review of this book.

But actually, reviews are really, really helpful. And that's the reason I ask.

See, the way the retailers work is they help potential readers to discover new books, *but only if those books have* recent *reviews*.

So if you liked this book and would like others to be able to discover it, please do take a moment right now to write a review and post it on the site of the retailer from which you got this book. It really does make a difference. Thank you.